THE **BATMAN** MOVIE™

RISE OF THE ROGUES

by **Beth Davies**

Batman created by Bob Kane with Bill Finger

Editor Pamela Afram
Designer Sam Bartlett
Senior Editor Hannah Dolan
Senior Designer Nathan Martin
Pre-production Producer Siu Yin Chan
Producer Louise Daly
Managing Editor Paula Regan
Design Managers Guy Harvey and Jo Connor
Publisher Julie Ferris
Art Director Lisa Lanzarini
Publishing Director Simon Beecroft

Batman created by Bob Kane with Bill Finger

First American Edition, 2017
Published in the United States by DK Publishing
345 Hudson Street, New York, New York 10014

Page design copyright © 2017 Dorling Kindersley Limited
DK, a Division of Penguin Random House LLC
17 18 19 20 10 9 8 7 6 5 4 3 2 1
001–297917–Jan/2017

A WORLD OF IDEAS:
SEE ALL THERE IS TO KNOW

www.dk.com
www.LEGO.com

Contents

4   Gotham City

6   The Hero Team

8   Commissioner Gordon

10   Meet the Rogues

12   The Joker

14   My Worst Enemy

16   Harley Quinn

18   The Joker's Notorious Lowrider

20   The Riddler

22   The Penguin

24   Mr. Freeze

26   Killer Croc

28   Catwoman

30   Poison Ivy

32   Clayface

34   The Joker's Plan

36   The Joker's Funhouse

38   Gotham City's Villains

40   Villains vs. the Hero Team

42   Locked Up

44   Quiz

46   Glossary

47   Guide for Parents

48   Index

Gotham City

Gotham City is a busy place, with lots of citizens.

Commissioner Jim Gordon is the Head of Police. It is his job to stop crime in the city.

Jim is soon going to retire from the job. His daughter, Barbara, is going to take over.

The Hero Team

Sometimes, Gotham City needs heroes! When a mission is too dangerous for the police alone, the police commissioner shines the Bat-Signal. Batman sees its light shining and rushes to the rescue. Batman likes to work alone, but sometimes he needs help. Robin and Batgirl help him to catch criminals and save the day. Three heroes are better than one!

COMMISSIONER JIM GORDON

— WANTS YOU TO HELP KEEP —

GOTHAM CITY SAFE

Citizens of Gotham City, please alert the police if you see any of the following:

 A **cat-like** woman prowling around jewelry stores.

 A man holding a giant **question mark**. Do not approach him! Conversation may cause confusion.

 A red-haired woman surrounded by wriggling **plants**.

 A man with a huge, **toothy grin**. Do not be fooled by his friendly appearance!

 GOTHAM CITY POLICE DEPARTMENT

 I BELIEVE IN BATMAN

KEEPING
GOTHAM CITY
SAFE

Meet the Rogues

Gotham City's villains have started working together, too. Their team is known as the Rogues.

Each of these crooks has fought Batman many times in the past. He has beaten each one alone, but never all of them at once! Batman will have to use all of his gadgets to save the day.

The Joker

The Joker is Batman's foe. He likes to cause trouble and create chaos in the city. The only thing that the Joker takes seriously is committing crime.

The Joker believes he is Batman's worst enemy. Batman does not agree. This wipes the smile off the Joker's face.

13

My <u>Worst</u> Enemy
by the Joker

Batman never laughs at my jokes, even though they are really funny!

He always tries to stop me from getting away from crime scenes.

He thinks he is really strong,
but I always have the last laugh!

Batman likes to take pictures
without me in them!

Harley Quinn

Harley Quinn is one
of the Joker's closest
allies. She loves his silly
pranks and nasty tricks.
Her colorful costume and
bright makeup are nearly
as eye-catching as the Joker's.

Harley used to be a doctor,
but now she causes chaos.
Batman should watch out
for her swinging bat.

The Joker's Notorious *Lowrider*

The car can bounce up and down

Silly golden chicken decoration

Wheels spinning at top speed

The Joker and Harley Quinn drive around Gotham City in the Joker's Notorious Lowrider. They create as much chaos as they can. This wacky vehicle looks harmless, but it is perfect for scaring people!

Music system hides button for missile launcher

Handles for Harley Quinn to grip on to while skating

A missile launcher is hidden inside the trunk

Horn to make people jump

The Riddler

One of the most confusing criminals in Gotham City is the Riddler. He leaves tricky puzzles at crime scenes for Batman to solve.

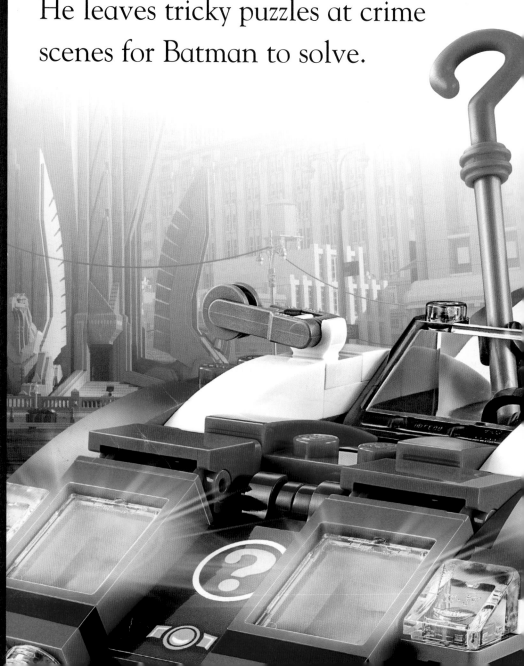

If Batman follows the tire tracks of the Riddler's Riddle Racer, he might be able to stop this Rogue once and for all. Or could this be another trick?

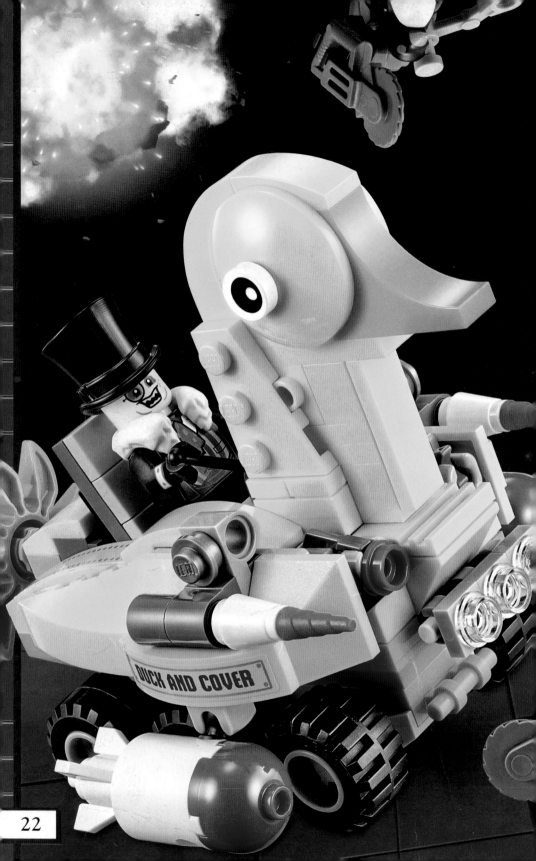

The Penguin

This businessman is no birdbrain! The Penguin controls lots of gangs in Gotham City. This has made him very rich. He wears an expensive top hat and suit.

The Penguin attacks Batman's Batcave with an army of penguin friends. His getaway vehicle is shaped like a duck.

Mr. Freeze

This frosty villain sends a chill
down Batman's spine. He wears
a large, armored suit that keeps
him ice-cold at all times.

Mr. Freeze is a scientist. He even
invented his own freeze gun.
He attacks the Gotham City
Energy Facility with the rest of the
Rogues. When he tells the scared
workers to "freeze," they really do!

Killer Croc

Killer Croc is one of Batman's most fearsome foes. He has a powerful tail, scaly skin, and snapping teeth—just like a real crocodile!

Killer Croc's truck is perfect
for driving through swamps.
It has large wheels and a big
headlight. Killer Croc controls
the vehicle from a section at the
back. He is so big, he cannot fit
in the driver's seat!

Catwoman

This crook is very good at breaking into buildings. Catwoman loves stealing from rich people in Gotham City. Her favorite things to steal are precious gems. This jewelry shop is a perfect target!

Catwoman makes a speedy getaway on her purple motorcycle. Luckily, Robin and Batgirl are right on her tail!

Poison Ivy

This Rogue likes plants much more than humans. Even her outfit is inspired by flowers. She has green-fingered gloves, and she wears leaves in her red hair.

Poison Ivy has special powers. She can control all forms of plant life. Poison Ivy wants to trap Batman in her tangling tendrils.

Clayface

Clayface is the biggest and messiest of Batman's foes. He is made of mud, and can transform into different shapes. He creates giant mud fists for attacking his enemies.

Clayface loves to destroy everything around him. Batman must watch out for the splats of mud he fires to stick people to the ground.

The Joker's Plan

The Joker is very smart. He has
come up with a cunning plan.
He wants to destroy Gotham City
Energy Facility, which supplies
all the power to the city. Gotham
City will be in total chaos and
the Joker will take over!

THE JOKER'S FUNHOUSE

Hi, everyone. It's the Joker! I have created my very own funhouse in Gotham City. Come inside. You won't be able to stop smiling. But you MUST follow these rules...

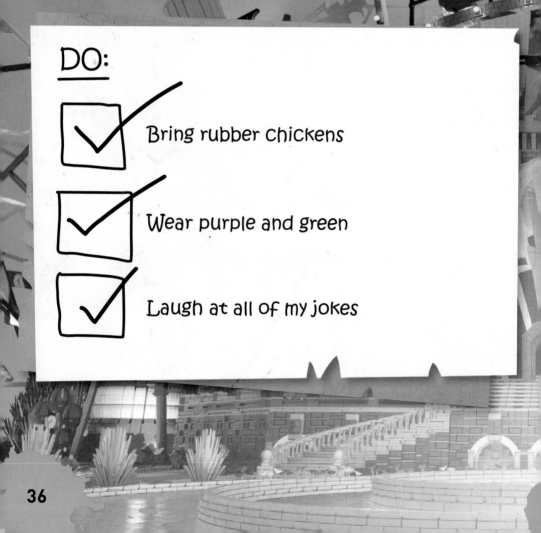

DO:

- ✓ Bring rubber chickens
- ✓ Wear purple and green
- ✓ Laugh at all of my jokes

DO NOT:

- [X] Wear black (or yellow)

- [X] Wear long black capes and drive bat-like vehicles

- [X] Wear black cowls with pointy ears

Gotham City's Villains

The Rogues aren't the only villains
in Gotham City. There are many
odd outlaws committing crimes.
There are villains dressed
as animals, like Zebra-Man,
March Harriet, and Orca.

The Mime

March Harriet

Orca

There are even villains who base their crimes on numbers, like The Calculator. All of these villains have one thing in common—they want to help the Joker defeat Batman!

Kite Man

The Eraser

Calendar
Man

The Calculator

Zebra-Man

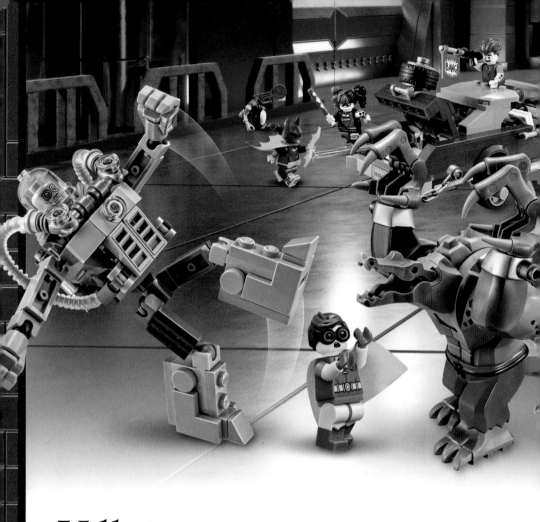

Villains vs.
the Hero Team

The Joker and his allies attack
the Gotham City Energy Facility!
It will take great teamwork for the
Hero Team to defeat the villains.

Batman takes on Clayface and
the Riddler. Robin tackles Mr.
Freeze and Killer Croc. Batgirl
battles with the Joker and Harley
Quinn. The Hero Team must win!

Locked Up

Hurrah! Batman, Batgirl, and Robin have put an end to the Joker's plan and defeated him.

All of the Rogues have been captured. They are now locked up in Arkham Asylum. Gotham City is safe once more. Thanks, Hero Team!

Quiz

1. Who is going to take over from Jim Gordon as Head of Police?

2. What kind of hat does the Penguin wear?

3. How does the police commissioner ask Batman for help?

4. How does Poison Ivy plan to trap Batman?

5. What kind of weapon does Harley Quinn use?

6. What is Catwoman's favorite thing to steal?

7. What does the Joker want to destroy?

8. Where are the Rogues now locked up?

Answers on page 48

Glossary

allies
A group of people who work together for a purpose.

Arkham Asylum
A hospital where Gotham's worst criminals are locked away.

citizen
Someone who lives in a town or city.

crook
A person who is dishonest or a criminal.

fearsome
Very frightening.

foe
An enemy or opponent.

gang
An organized group of criminals.

scientist
A person who studies science and solves problems by doing experiments.

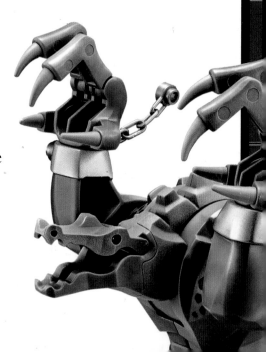

Guide for Parents

This book is part of an exciting four-level reading series for children, developing the habit of reading widely for both pleasure and information. These chapter books have a compelling main narrative to suit your child's reading ability. Each book is designed to develop your child's reading skills, fluency, grammar awareness, and comprehension in order to build confidence and engagement when reading.

Ready for a *Level 2* book

YOUR CHILD SHOULD

- be familiar with using beginning letter sounds and context clues to figure out unfamiliar words.
- be aware of the need for a slight pause at commas and a longer one at periods.
- alter his/her expression for questions and exclamations.

A VALUABLE AND SHARED READING EXPERIENCE

For many children, reading requires much effort, but adult participation can make this both fun and easier. So here are a few tips on how to use this book with your child.

TIP 1 **Check out the contents together before your child begins:**

- read the text about the book on the back cover.
- flip through the book and stop to chat about the contents page together to heighten your child's interest and expectation.
- make use of unfamiliar or difficult words on the page in a brief discussion.
- chat about the nonfiction reading features used in the book, such as headings, captions, lists, or charts.